A rainbow to teach children all about different types of crystals.

Red: Carnelian is a stone used for motivation, endurance, leadership, and courage. Carnelian gives you the drive to go after what you want in life. The color of Carnelian can vary from red to a reddish brown.

Orange: Amber is fossilized tree resin. Amber is used for suppressing depression, stimulates intellect, promotes self-confidence, and creative self-expression. The color of Amber can vary from orange to yellow, red, black, brown, blue, and green. There are sometimes insects inside.

Yellow: Citrine is from the Quartz family. Citrine is used to gain wealth, higher knowledge, health, and bliss. The color of Citrine can vary from yellow to a golden brown.

Green: Fluorite is a stone used for healing and protection. The color of Fluorite can vary widely. Fluorite comes in green, purple, blue, white, pink, yellow, red, brown, grey, black, colorless, multi-colored and banded as well.

Blue: Lapis Lazuli is a stone used for wisdom and truth. This crystal has a beautiful deep blue color with flecks of gold and brown throughout.

Indigo: Blue Tiger's Eye is a stone used for protection against ill wishes, as well as useful for memory, and helping you get what you really want.

Violet: Amethyst is a stone often used for relieving stress and sadness, as well as for dispelling anger, rage, fear, and doubt. Amethyst comes in a wide range of purple shades.

White: Howlite is a stone used for patience, relieving rage, pain, and stress. Howlite encourages emotional expression. The colors of natural Howlite are white with gray, black, or dark brown veining.

Brown: Bronzite is a stone used to promote peace, and harmony, while helping with forgiveness and compassion. The colors of Bronzite are a deep bronze brown and they have red and golden patches throughout.

Black: Black Obsidian is a stone naturally formed by cooled volcanic lava. Obsidian is used for protection, grounding, and healing. The colors of obsidian are black, tan, or green. Rarely Obsidian is found as red, blue, orange, or yellow.

Rainbow: Rainbow Aura Quartz is a stone used for clearing negative and stressful energy, as well as replacing negative energy with loving, positive vibrations. Use Rainbow Aura to increase the abilities of other crystals.

All of these crystals make up a beautiful rainbow of metaphysical help.